Good Morning, I Love You

by V. Rose

Edited by Yvette Rebello

Book Cover by KEVA Graphics Studio

Formatted by Vellichor Ink

Interior images by CanvaPro

First edition 2025

For Ren, Syd, Caleb, and Amber,
for being my rocks in your own ways.

For Kristi, because you were right, the world needs a real story
of grief and love.

Authors Note

Death is inevitable, and the journey ahead takes us all through pretzel-twisted roller-coaster rides, but we should not be alone. The collective of those left behind, all dressed in joyous memories, shall walk the path hand in hand.

Since I completed this project, I have carried the memories forward to the world we dreamed of together, and more, with my four children and two grandchildren.

Never alone.

Compendium

Good Morning, I Love You

Not Alone
Healing with the
Recollection of Love

by V. Rose

The Dawn of Grief

I greeted the world with anger and hate. Trembling, my hand closed our front door behind me. As I walked toward the car, the rustling pile of leaves on the ground annoyed me. The autumn smell stirred my being. It was the first time I left the house without kissing Silly's forehead with a *See you later* or sending a quick text saying *I am leaving for work*. His smile, quirks, and "Good morning, I love yous" swirled in my head.

His hammock still hung under the ghoulish naked branches of the Bradford pear tree. "The fish tree" we called it. The sleepy sun shone at the home we built together. I climbed into the silver Subaru he didn't get a chance to upgrade and never would. The bag from the hospital sat quietly on the floorboard. I reached for the last T-shirt he wore.

"I can't wait to go see *Wicked* next week. I don't think I will have a problem walking up to the nose-bleed seats we got. I should celebrate my new height and wear my utility kilt!" he'd excitedly said two days before he left this world. We were on the way home from the hospital after his successful elective back surgery. Early autumn, our favorite season. Looking for his scent, I stuffed my face in the old T-shirt and held back tears so as not to soil the last bit of him on the piece of fabric.

My favorite month was turning into the darkest era of my life ahead of my forty-third birthday.

Within twenty minutes, seven traffic lights, and two towns, our stories from the past surfaced with anguish.

"We are going to have our Thanksgiving in our new kitchen this year."

I recalled the smile on his face when he said that at the hospital during his recovery. Accepting the fact my Thanksgiving would no longer be what it would have been with him, I freely let my tears flow. I couldn't even continue with the renovation. The resentment of not being able to make more memories triggered a searing pain. Between sobs, I replayed event after event.

I missed his *I love you so much! I don't even care if you don't have any boobs!* His silliness that birthed the endearing name I gave him: Silly. The way he said things, the calm in his uniquely funny ways.

Born with pulmonary hemitruncus, a high mortality rate congenital heart disease in the 70s, he'd won the challenges his life presented. My mind couldn't wrap my head around his finale.

I parked my car under a massive pine tree. I wanted to turn around and return to my dark and quiet place among layers of blankets and his pillows. When I wiped my tears and convinced myself to stay, a warmth of comfort surrounded me.

"I am always proud of you. You light up any room you enter," he often said in my nervousness.

The breeze whispered for me to keep going. I felt lifted as I stepped out into the space I'd not been in for a couple of months. That day I went back to work as a widow, an unkind status.

Not long after the day my life became a stranger, a few ladies around me lost their partners. Helpless, I opted to share the memories that frequently visited me. Verbalizing them with Moni and Astrid comforted me. Our conversations, rejoicing our memories, brought waves of unexpected, reciprocal healing energy. A couple of them reached out to me frequently just for an understanding ear or to reminisce on random, meaningful memories we had with our loved ones. In return, I reached out to them to make sure they never felt the loneliness I often felt. My healing door was ajar, and the invitation was painfully appealing.

This scribble began as my way to channel my anguish and pain. With time, it became my oxygen to carry on in the absence of a partnership, a friendship, and a shared life. With each memory I penned, the brighter the joy he brought into my life. It was such a twist to find the pain of resurfacing memories morphed into my healing beacon. His gift of perspective, kindness, and courage became a compass to navigate the complexities of life after the moment that changed everything. Forcing myself to enter the healing door, I greeted those memories, and with them, I found two new friends: renewed hope and a rediscovered me.

Good morning. Love

Hollow Mornings

"You know the Bible never says exactly when mornings start."

He was adamant that the Bible never mentioned the exact hour of a new day. For over four thousand days the routine was as predictable as the sunrise itself. In the last few years, his morning started at around ten a.m. Then he would text or call me with a *Good morning, I love you*. Some days I beat him to it, especially if I needed him to wake up for chores or appointments.

Being in bed alone, I rolled over to find him many mornings. His ringtone and notifications stopped coming. The blanket was undisturbed and cold. My eyes opened and my mind was burdened. The absence of his sleepy glances effaced the sweetest cheer for the day ahead. Had I taken for granted our wordless exchanges? Running my hand over his pillow often, I looked for something, anything. I wanted him to be there. Reclosing my eyes, I wanted to wake up from this nightmare.

For the first few months, I swam and drowned in a fog. My friend, sleep, left me. The guilt and what-ifs lingered everywhere I turned. My own voice screamed at me. *You let him die!* replayed in my head. A long list of should-haves replaced my music playlist and work to-do list. Exhaustion swallowed me from the long stretch of two-hour sleep.

He was cheerful and full of hope the night we did not expect to be his last. We arrived home the day before that and celebrated his remarkable recovery with dinner and laughter. We had the two youngest kids working on homework and sharing their days with Dad. Despite his request for me to stay with him in his temporary recovery room in my downstairs office, I hugged him and kissed him good night.

"I don't want to hurt you," I said.

A mere twelve hours later I was mopping the hospital floor with my tearful face. The last smile I saw on his face before I headed upstairs that night was a gift.

It was tough to find the strength to get up and face the day. Simple things like taking a shower or getting dressed were huge tasks. His warm sleepy look and morning snoring used to signal the start of my day. The void of it confined me to the quiet stillness of our bed. Would he be alive if I had slept with him that night? I only wanted him to be comfortable in his bed. I should have checked on him first before I showered that day. On and on with the *should have's*. When I peeked into the room, he looked so peaceful, like always. I thought I was giving him a few more minutes of sleep. Our youngest's "What's wrong with Dad?" rang continuously in my head. Never could I have I imagined my fourteen-year old would be the one to find her dad unconscious.

When the kids' alarm interrupted one of the silent morning, I had no choice but to drag myself out of bed. Though hazy, their needs were still my top priority. I felt like a robot going through the motions. My heart and mind still reminisced about the life that once was whole.

My reflection in the mirror jolted a realization in me. Who was this tired and empty girl staring back at me? The vibrant spirit escaped my eyes. They were hollow. My smile, which Silly said lit up the room, had vanished. The energetic mom my kids needed could not be found.

The empty pantry reminded me of my unfinished task. It snapped me out of my dark and chaotic state. The lingering backache from spending hours curled up in bed could not be ignored. The unfamiliar smell of my neglected self was rotting. I stepped out of the grief bubble. For the sake of my kids and myself, I took a step to move forward. Despite the heartache, my kids needed and deserved some normalcy. The road ahead was uncertain, but I couldn't deny the need to begin.

Facing the stranger in the reflection, I saw a painful clarity. I told myself that I needed to come back to reality. Moving forward was the promise we made to each other. We vowed to persevere through the darkest storms. The time had come to renew that pledge. It was time to rebuild the part of him that lived on in our children's laughter, mischievous smiles, and kind actions.

I made a choice that hollow morning. He was not there and only I could manage the nightmare. I appreciated his adamance that we should be able to choose when our days started. My precious Silly and his wisdom of time. I chose the time when my day would start when I was ready, and it was now.

I hope you feel the winds
on your skin today

Bitter Creamy Medium Roast

The gentle dawn used to embrace me with a familiar ritual. Half a cup of sugar, cream, and a drop of coffee started my days. On his days off from work, my Silly would remain in bed until his morning began. Unlike me and my coffee, his caffeine ritual came in a cold green bottle. While I embraced my work and weekend chores early, when his calendar was open, he would start slowly and steadily around midday.

It was not only habits and preferences that drove our varied morning routines. Our work demanded a unique blend of daily patterns. He transitioned from a comfortable eight-to-five technology career to a first responder working twenty-four- to forty-eight-hour shifts. Our work and parenting schedules created a caffeine-loaded household. For a period of time, our moshed schedule divided our home. It became a space where our quirks clashed with exhaustion and frustration. We tripped over our habits, and annoyance ensued.

The following days after he passed, I missed some of those quirky arguments and flirtatious make-up moments. I so vividly wanted him to reach around my waist and stop me from getting up too early. I wanted to annoy him by making a morning ruckus before he was ready to get up.

Those disruptions and mix-match routines introduced us to the delicate art of ritual compromise. Over time, we discovered ways to share our symphony of dawn and daybreak. Our routines softened and we adapted. I enjoyed my morning brew while he had his extra snooze. Many Saturdays, I rejoined him in bed for extra cuddles under the cozy covers, followed by our divide-and-conquer approach to weekend chores. Other times we opted for lazy time past noon. Those precious morning hugs, those fleeting moments of solace, became the beautiful rhythm that set the tone for our entire day.

Those routines sailed with him in his final slumber. As the sun rose each day since, I longed for those stolen connections. I yearned to hear his sweet whispers and feel the warmth of his embrace. Those seemingly ordinary moments were our love story.

It was about finding a new routine. In a rebellious act against my predictable sweet cravings, I let the creamer flood my coffee and ignored the crystalized sweetener. The initial bitter taste shocked my taste buds. The unfriendly taste with each sip confirmed a change. My bitter new routine sat before the dim glow of my work monitor. It mirrored the essence of my current state, life without him. He was the sweetness I longed for, the dissolved crystals of joy in my otherwise plain existence.

Sunrise upon sunrise I distanced myself from my old ways. I tried different coffees and creamers with sugar untouched.

It was a change since those days when he commented, "Are you drinking coffee or coffee-flavored sugar?" I explored the diverse blend of caffeinated beans. Some days I detoured to coffee joints and broke the monotony of break-room coffee. With my stimulant adventures, I have grown to love the tint of bitterness. It was my adaptation to the raw honesty of life's current flavors. Every morning, with the first sip of something new, I celebrated the past while embracing the solitary journey ahead. And in the ever-changing landscape of my cup, the absence of sweetness held a piece of him with me. He will always be my sweetener.

I hung on to our routines for a while. It was easier to adjust my schedule with him there despite the challenges. Our adaptation together had a purpose: us, our family. When I opened my life to healing, it took me some time. As I learned to change how I took my coffee, I learned to embrace a new routine. I embraced an unsweetened journey.

When you're ready, try
something new

Chocolate Vs. Vanilla

"I can't always be the target of dumbassery. I have a much greater purpose in life." Silly and his special wisdom as he entered the house on September 12th, 2001.

One early Autumn day, when the planes struck the Twin Towers, my Silly was on the receiving end of some unkind words from a manager. While the breaking news covered the loss of thousands of lives, he was fixing a broken computer from a floppy disk inserted backward and upside down. The memory of him walking into the house that day was so vivid. He was working his EMT clinical a short few months after, leaving his prestigious technology career behind.

He was born rambunctiously wise. His compassion and acceptance of human conditions multiplied since he donned his uniform. I supposed his perspective shifted with all the things he saw in his field. He captured people's attention with his insight which he delivered so effortlessly. While he lived, I rolled my eyes at those bits of wisdom; they now stuck with me like tiny seeds planted in the depths of my mind. His echoing voice guided me through tough times without him physically by my side.

One of his profound words of wisdom was about the seemingly trivial choice between chocolate and vanilla ice cream. It seemed insane when we had the conversation then. I may have even been dismissive of it. Time cracked open my shell and shifted my perspective. I started to understand the truth behind his words.

"Why do you think vanilla is the best ice cream?" he asked. My response was always that I just loved vanilla. He argued how could I judge the only thing I tried as the best. By definition, best is the top rank of many. I sat on that for quite a while. Mint chocolate then became my favorite ice cream flavor. It was a constant reminder that life's most important decisions can be found in the seemingly mundane act of trying.

It was that simple question that pushed me to explore new horizons, to take risks, and to grow as an individual. We continued these little nuggets of wisdom with our children and friends. They were met with eye rolls or shrugs often but most of them stuck. They had used his wisdom more times than they'd care to admit. Unknowingly, they have relied on it when faced with uncertainty and the fear of trying something new. As an observer, I witnessed his teachings applied by many around us. Their growth and self-discovery came from venturing beyond what is familiar.

As the historical event of the September Eleventh made him love being a medic, my grief made me seek a new flavor in life. I got back on my feet, I found myself trying new "ice cream flavors" in ways of new adventures, new hobbies, and new ways of living. Some of them I probably wouldn't repeat. I also stumbled upon something I came to love. Out of all things artistic, I started pottery. I wore outfits I would have never worn before. I did my hair differently and got tattoos of all kinds of things. And the biggest one yet: here I was, writing to share the same wisdom with the world.

Among the explorations, I also found that the variation we crave is not just about new things. I revisited what I hadn't done for a while. I found a new love for the little things I already loved. Those subtle differences became a whole new world awaiting. When we dared to step beyond our comfort zone, we embraced the essence of how life becomes as rich and diverse as the flavors we have yet to savor.

Be in your moment

Roses Never Died

U nlike our whimsical fantasies, the earlier chapters of our life together were written with a frugal hand. We had to make necessities a luxury. Our early days focused on honing our survival instincts. We pinched pennies for groceries, paid bills diligently, and made sure the lights stayed on, and the water ran warm.

Being a paramedic was not as fancy as it was depicted on those various TV shows. Being a uniformed serviceman meant taking a significant pay cut from working in the glamorous technology business. The weekly steak house visits were replaced with whatever protein was on sale and cheap pizza Fridays. Parties and boozy weekends turned to intimate family movie or game nights.

Adapting to a frugal lifestyle was an exciting challenge for me. Not so much for Silly. He had to learn to value things differently. His gift-giving love language needed a new approach. He became a more conscious buyer with research and discerning eyes.

I swam in my spreadsheets with meticulous budgeting. I thought I knew every cent that flowed through them. Later, I found out he had been setting money aside to speak his language of love for me and the kids. He often spontaneously surprised me with fresh flowers or other simply beautiful gifts. They added a rare hue of splendor to our carefully budgeted life.

When he worked his first responder schedule, I didn't see him much at home when he was not exhausted. I vividly remember the day he took a quick drive to my work. He walked in with a big smile and a bouquet of fresh roses. They looked expensive; I knew they were. I was grateful yet concerned. I hated that he spent money on something that would die in a short time. Often, I was ungrateful and unkind when accepting his gifts. There were times I made him feel guilty for spending the money.

I carefully turned the bouquet upside down to dry and to preserve them. I kept the dried bouquets on display for weeks. I wanted him to know I still had them, and he didn't have to spend money to buy another for a while.

Looking back at those moments, I regretted my selfish and negative reactions. My unkindness not only hurt him but also myself. It took away the joy he had in giving. I longed to bring those sweet moments back. I was so focused on being financially responsible that I failed to appreciate him.

In recent times, I've found that a simple phrase of "thank you" holds so much weight. It's a genuine expression of gratitude. When I said it, there was no "but" lurking in the shadows, just pure appreciation. Moreover, the amazing feeling of seeing him candidly in the least expected moments taught me to do unto others. As I recalled the joy of seeing him unexpectedly, I accustomed myself to reaching out or showing up for others who'd crossed my mind. It became a symbol of learned grace and a tribute to his enduring spirit of giving. I began to keep the roses alive within me and paid them forward instead of keeping them dry. Admired loudly and visibly. Not buts, no excuses, just a simple *thank you* sufficed.

Give yourself grace

Topless Wrangler to Odyssey

Born with a complex congenital heart disease and no guarantee future, Silly started a family early. Open-heart surgery at five months old shaped a person and their supporting family. He used to say that he needed to live it up "before his time lapsed". With his first partnership, he brought two amazing kids into my life. The oldest daughter, Booger Bear and her little brother, Little Man, were staying with their mother full-time when I met him. We saw them periodically. The earlier stage of suddenly "with children" was an ice-cold shock to me. Yes, I took the chance with them anyway, even more so because he shared his love for these babies on our very first date. That very minute I saw his true color, his humanism, and his character.

Time helped us figure out how to navigate the complexities of a blended family. Gradually, it shaped my role in their lives. We cherished our time with the young ones; those were moments we looked forward to. The kids' laughter filled our home, making it a sanctuary of shared memories and new traditions. Despite the intricacies of our situation, the love that grew between us was undeniable, becoming an integral part of our family unit.

When I met Silly, he thought he was inching toward what he called his "expiration date." We focused on living. At the same time, his choice to start a family early as part of living created responsibility. The decision tied him down from an early age. It shaped his youth into a mosaic of obligations and mature decisions. In the midst of it all, our story had an undeniable zest for life. When we found ourselves alone together, we lived it up. During one of these lively moments, an opportunity came up. A friend offered to trade his beat-up car with ours, which turned into an unexpected adventure. Without hesitation, Silly said yes to an aged, hunter-green 1985 Wrangler. It was a beast with signs of time and neglect. A tangible challenge that demanded our attention was exactly what we didn't know we needed. This project was an endeavor that needed a whole lot of love and maintenance.

The Wrangler, the Beast, became his dearest project. Piece by piece, he decked it out. This project brought me close to his family. While Silly, his brother in-love, and nephew got dirty in the garage, I spent quite a bit of time with the ladies, my then-future niece and sister in-love.

His work brought the beautiful beast to roar. With its rugged embrace, we embarked on adventures. His research throughout the entire project also brought him new friends. Alone or with the crowd, we took his motorized baby driving freely through rushing rivers and rock piles. With it, we conquered rough terrain and muddy paths. The joy of our journey echoed in every spin of the wheels. It was during these adrenaline-fueled escapades that the Wrangler also became a catalyst for our expanding family. It jostled and nudged the

onset of my first pregnancy's contractions. It was a serendip-
itous push that came two weeks past the due date. That adventure preempted the welcoming of our first child together
into the world.

The birth of our Peep meant it was time to grow up again.
With the arrival of their little sister, Booger Bear and Little
Man moved in with us. Suddenly stepping back into the role
of a full-time dad of three, change was inevitable. With a
heavy heart but a clear determination, he bid farewell to his
off-road companion. The story would remain in our hearts;
the adventures and significant life moments we shared. Beast
was parked for a while. Then, in its place, a family minivan
rolled into our lives. It marked the end of an era and the
beginning of another, where the hum of an engine tuned for
reliability replaced the roar of our wild joyrides. This memory
encapsulated the evolution of our family journey.

The true meaning of it all eluded me, a blind spot in a story
rich with emotion and sacrifice. Looking back now, I wish I
had understood the weight of his decision and the depth of
his reasoning. It may have seemed like a simple and practical
choice, but it was so much more. It was an intentional decision, a silent testament to his priorities. We, his family, were
the center of his world. Our safety and comfort came first,
soaring above his personal joyrides and daring adventures.

Be Well

Organism

When time allowed, we held our family dinners around the table dearly. If only our dining table could retell the stories. The idiosyncrasy in our evening conversation spoke uniquely about who we were as individuals. The kids loved their dad's "I get no respect!" He used that phrase in part seriousness and part jokingly when someone took his favorite piece of meat, or if the kids got to the last of his favorite dishes. When the kids got older, they would say it to their dad before he said it to them.

The time around the table continued beyond dinner. It was an unwritten agreement that when we gathered around the table, we could talk freely. Questions, hard and easy, had been asked around the table. Lessons, disagreements, and pure moments of letting go of what was bottled up inside. Silly was a great listener. To all the kids, he was the encyclopedia of both useful and useless knowledge. He was a master storyteller.

When Silly and I began our family, we built a covenant of trust and safety. We made it known to our kids that they should never feel scared to ask for help for themselves or their friends. Our home was a gathering place for our children and their friends. In our kitchen, we prepared many meals for them, especially those with absent guardians. A strong sentiment we shared: Kids should never feel alone and hungry.

One evening, Booger Bear had a few girls over for dinner. They were all in middle school at the time. When I usually started to clear the table, Silly would normally get up and continue his evening with a book or game. Not that night! The pink-cheeked, giggly teenagers asked him to stay for some questions. I recalled so vividly watching them from behind the kitchen counter, asking him to clarify a few things they'd learned at their recent sex-education lesson at school.

"Yeah, so how do we know what an 'organism' is like?" One of the girls embarrassedly whispered. Silly tilted his head, puzzled at what she meant.

"You know, *organism*," they all repeated in unison.

The other girls jumped in to help describe the word in question and it was as chaotic as a game of Scattergories. He burst into laughter, and his hand hit the table a few times as his pale face turned beat red. He looked at my confused self.

"Orgasm! You want to know what orgasm is?" his thunderous voice filled the room. I cried with laughter.

He had a similar conversation three more times after that, one with each child as they hit puberty. None was as funny as the first. That evening was the only time we used "organism" in this context.

His patience and ways of explaining even the most sensitive topics were beyond me. He listened well. Even though his "stern dad voice" was not the kids' favorite, they loved sharing everything with him. He created such a clear boundary, and the limit was simple: no lies. Quick to forgive, he took time to talk with reason.

None of us were ever perfect, but with his declining medical conditions, his patience often wore thin. Irritability visited him often. Short fuses required him to have more time to breathe, listen, and respond. But one thing remained the same, he welcomed openness and curiosity. I wished I were a fly on the wall during those conversations he had with the kids. I became the recipient of those wisdoms through my children. In a time of need, one of the kids would throw out a healing phrase only their dad would ever say. They had the power of verbalizing our big emotions and hunger for knowledge, wrong words and all.

Have a tiny smile today

Never Bland

Our backgrounds were so different that on some days, I felt like a character straight out of a storybook. Our narrative was shaped by the clash and mash of my Indonesian story and Silly's good ol' southern boy upbringing. Our journey together broke down judgments and illuminated the shadows of understanding. We navigated through the tapestry of diversity with patience and open hearts. With it, we found that love speaks a language that knows no boundaries. Our different histories built a bridge that connected our worlds. Our openness constructed a safe haven for our family and the people around us.

There was no guarantee on how the medical procedure he had done as a baby would prolong his life. Since I met him, his family was always fearful of his tentatively short life. His close-knit southern family loved, protected, and sheltered him. In the culinary aspect of things, however, they helped him commit a serious crime. He only knew to eat his steak well done and serve only the driest salt and pepper turkey.

When we first met, he expressed to me how some things I shared were bizarre to him. The food I ate seemed odd. My tradition was alien to his family and vice versa. It took both of us time to adapt and assimilate. I opened my mind to his upbringing and family culture as he opened his to mine and the world through our shared holidays and large family gatherings.

My first American thanksgiving was the southern sort. Stacked paper plates next to a homemade potato salad and collard greens, surrounded by his family and their adult jokes. I learned to cook that day. Every year since, I made the best turkey in the family, or so he said. Especially as I introduced the big bird to various worldly spices.

On our earlier dates, seafood and eggs were also a big no-no for him. One special evening in the beautiful and freezing Michigan autumn, we had our first fancy dinner. Teased by the delicious smells from the nearby restaurants, our stomachs protested as we explored the charming downtown streets of Ann Arbor. A decadent scent invited us to a fancy steak house. Silly being a single dad and me, a college student, the menu was a bit pricey for either of us. We made a prudent pact to share an entrée, with his steak cooked to a level that I could actually enjoy, paired with some shrimp for him to try. No more chewy steak or dry turkey for him since.

In our blended family, we agreed to let our children savor the rich flavors of our diverse heritages. We were a "garden salad" type of family. Our home was a plateful of mixed characters and personalities. We learned important lessons, made necessary adjustments, and embraced each other's idiosyncrasies. We recognized how our disagreements were crucial for our family's growth, collectively and individually. We created an environment to allow our children to appreciate the beautiful blend of flavors. The mash of characters included beliefs and life's approaches. There was no judgment before we tried, no prejudice before we sought to understand.

Claiming that before he was southern, he was partly an Irishman, we started an Irish tradition for St. Paddy's Day. My first attempt at making an easy-cooked, traditional corned beef and cabbage was one to never forget. Unlike the calming scent around Thanksgiving, the corned beef and cabbage aroma greeted our home quite offensively. Giggles erupted as the children playfully wrinkled their noses, and our son teased, "I wonder if Irish houses smell like farts once a year like this?" Laughter filled the house. Yes, laughter was the best seasoning for open-mindedness.

As we journeyed through life, we agreed to be open and explore. We learned that the people we met were our equals. Our adventures took us to try local flavors and embrace the culture of every place we visited. Food was more than just fuel, it was a powerful bond that brought people together. It fostered both understanding and acceptance. With every bite, we were not just having a meal. We were savoring the essence of a place and its people. We spread love and appreciation across our table and beyond. The new things, both the ones we enjoyed and those we would not have again, seasoned our lives from being bland.

Feel your feels

Kayak and Hammock

Our love created a space where we felt safe together with life's ups and downs. At the same time, we allowed corners of solitude for us to be our own individual selves. He claimed his peace in the house, while I enjoyed being lost in the graceful sway of trees and the beautiful songs of birds. His books and video games were his comfort company, while dirt and running water were mine.

A few weeks before our first born, Peep, turned one, a major life change happened. Silly came home early from work. Entering the house, he had a bottle of gelatinous red liquid he had coughed up. We rushed to a couple of different emergency rooms to no avail. We reached out to the hospital three hours away that saved his life at five months old and had retained hundreds of his medical records. Despite the offer for a convalescent ambulance or medi-helicopter to pick him up, the stubborn man I married preferred driving. He kept his uniform on; one hand on the steering wheel and the other tightly holding the bloody bottle. On Peep's first birthday, they removed his right lung to stop the bleeding.

All that came with a loss of an organ changed our habits, our lives. His indoor routine was no longer conducive for his mental health that was a product of the surgery he'd endured.

His body demanded natural light. His singular lung craved the plant-produced oxygen and its natural circulation. His migration to the outdoors brought us proximity. The increase of his presence in my outdoor space was calming. Though many times we kept in our own quiet space, being in each other's orbit brought comfort. Glancing at him lying in his hammock or sitting on our porch chair while I gardened or plucked weeds lifted my spirits. The unspoken companionship connected our existence.

And then there was the kayak. Introduced to us by a friend, the molded plastic became his new friend. The water delivered an allure of peace. The soothing sound of passing boats created gentle ripples to softly rock and sway his existence. He found himself drawn to the rhythmic strokes of the oars and the peaceful solitude of the river. He discovered a new space on the water. The peace of nothing but the vast blue sky above and the mirrored surface below elevated his healing. The serenity of kayaking took him to a place where the chaos of life turned into a beautiful flow.

What was once my world had become his, and more. It was his dream to paddle down a river a few hours away from us and finish at the great ocean. Despite the challenges his health posed, the river called to him. He gripped onto the promising journey with the relaxing twists of inland waterways to the vast embrace of the sea. His destiny had a different plan. Long after his pneumonectomy, his heart was failing. Kayaking became physically tougher. Cheering and supporting him, we equipped the family with extra kayaks. We kept him company for his safety and to provide help. At some point we made his long kayak journey to the ocean our shared vision. Together, it was a future expedition our family aspired to undertake. The thought of the river's current leading us to the shorelines of the mighty ocean filled us with hope and excitement.

There were moments where life's schedule got in the way. When we couldn't go, and he couldn't put the kayak in the river alone, he found ways to mimic the gentle sway of the water. He found a spot between two trees at the front of our house. His hammock swung between the sturdy oaks. The leaf-dappled sky entertained him. The gentle swing echoed the soft bobbing of the kayak. Surrounded by whispers of the wind and touched by the flickering sunlight, he would find relief and rest his eyes. His spirit navigated the calm tides of resilience.

We did not get to paddle the Neuse River to the Atlantic. I deeply believed that he was traveling that river pain-free in his new universe. Carrying his hammock pouch everywhere now became a constant reminder of his strength and resilience through life's ups and downs. Moments when his absence gripped me, the hammock threads brought comfort, holding onto precious memories. Just like he found peace under the oak trees, I held onto a piece of his haven. It's not just fabric and rope; it's a legacy that gave me the courage to face challenges head-on knowing I had something to rest on in tough times. The open sky and nature's sounds reminded me of his calm presence.

May the butterfly meet you today

Beyond Sexcapade

The first six years of being parents were immersed in the chaos of little feet scampering and barking at any dynamics we had. Our moments as a couple, when neither one of us was tired, were rare. Four kids and three fur babies completed our family. Intimacy and couple-moments were, however, absorbed by the overwhelming mayhem. The ebb and flow of our everyday routine gradually pulled us apart. It was not a sudden blow. Unfortunately, it was a subtle distance, leaving behind a faint whisper of the unity we once shared.

As dual-working parents, the weight of it all often felt unbearable. There were a few stretches of time when the gap between us grew wider. Exhaustion from parenting and working consumed every fiber of our being. Days turned into weeks, and some days our interactions felt superficial. Those tough moments made our relationship transactional rather than the deep connections we were used to. It was astonishing how fragile intimacy became unnoticed tired silences and unexpressed desires. We drifted apart frequently. Two souls yearning for each other amid the deafening noise of life's demands. It was so deep that others couldn't even see it.

In the intricate fabric of our lives, however, it was those little cracks of trouble that strangely brought us closer. I secretly
thank the universe for the unexpected occasions that reignited
our bond. It was the screech of moments effortlessly cutting
through the noise of our daily lives that reminded us of our
profound connection. Looking back, the challenges that once
felt like insurmountable mountains turned out to be mere
bumps on our journey as a couple. They were small triggers
that pushed us back together. Such fascination at the very
obstacles we wanted to avoid, ended up being the catalysts
that reunited us.

Between the burdening responsibilities, we paused to find
what we were missing. We missed our weekend getaways and
our reconnecting time. Those precious breaks from the per-
petual chaos granted us a chance to reflect and reconnect.
It could be a cozy cottage, or a ready-made tent nestled in
nature's embrace where we could disconnect. Even if it was
just an hour away from home, we enjoyed the feeling of stepping into an entirely different world. In that simple cocoon
of quietness, we indulged in him-and-me time. For a few
hours, we had no lunch boxes to pack, and no letting out
animals for potty time. Those twenty-four-hour getaways,
or even the fortunate forty-eight-hour ones, became lifelines.
Those moments allowed us to rediscover each other. Oh, the
conversations we had. We delved deeper into the intricacies of
our souls. Each escape taught me something new; about him,
about myself, and about the unique dance we shared.

Just a mere five years after his pneumonectomy, the doctor
delivered the much-feared C word. It was Silly's second throat

cancer diagnosis. He never smoked or used tobacco products in his life. Months prior to this dreadful news, we argued daily. We screamed and fought over nothing more than money. The often-unresolved financial challenges kept us awake with anger. We held each other's hand on the way home from the appointment. We called a friend to take care of the kids. We packed our clothes and in silence, we drove up to a cabin in the mountains. Yes, we spent the money we argued about. We also spent that weekend laughing at how silly the past two months had been. I left my job soon after and took a pay cut to be closer to home. We scheduled nonnegotiable date nights. We celebrated his remission a year later.

Before Silly died, we were blessed with a couple of weeks of quality time at the hospital while he was recovering from his back surgery. Recalling it, we laughed about our sexcapades. I was grateful to know that being a mom didn't overshadow my role as a wife. They went hand in hand in life. The tough times spotlighted a relationship balance before it slipped away. It cherished the delicate harmony of being both parents and partners.

And so, my journey went on. Here I was riding the ever-changing rhythm of life. I cherished the memories of those weekend getaways. The power of connection and the mysterious chaos that helped nurture connection and growth. Always, I believed there were always reasons!

It's okay to nap today

As Intended

I did not last two weeks being a stay-at-home mom after giving birth to Peep. If we were to compare our stay-at-home parenting resume, my Silly won the best, most gentle dad award. Especially as it related to brushing the girls' hair and trimming our son's locks. Silly-1, me-0.

Being the safe haven, I knew better. He had more struggles than he allowed the world to see. When he hung up his suits and ties for a medic uniform, he imagined rescuing lives as long as he was breathing. He did not expect to live forever, but he also did not expect to not be able to serve at all while alive. The burden of damaged pride as a dad and a man was insurmountable. Our kids loved him, but as his physical pain worsened, so did his mental wellness.

Chub's birth celebrated his strength and courage. It was also a gift that fueled his daily excitement after hanging up his uniform. The baby ,who many said was a copy of me, was a light that brought him out of the darkness. Though she did not replace his sense of purposelessness, she anchored him with her silliness and wild personality.

One evening, he asked for some "him time." I went upstairs to bathe the baby. While reaching for the washcloth behind me, my newborn decided to turn and dunk her head in the water— I did say she was wild! I rushed to pick her up as she struggled to cough, and her complexion turned blue. I screamed in utter panic. Silly climbed up the stairs, removed the baby from me, and gently but surely turned her over and forced her to cough. She did, and it was followed by one of her biggest grins. Watching him rock her against his chest as she cooed, the feeling was indescribable.

A few weeks before he died, next to him at the hospital bed during his recovery turned out to be our last quality time together. We talked about time, purpose, and being a part of the great art of the universe. He squeezed my hand recalling how his years in medicine were not in vain. His preparedness to rescue our child was a purpose we never would have written in our predictive story.

Trial and tribulation shaped his faith as my curiosity and privilege shaped mine. I loved our arguments and disagreements on the subject. It always delivered reflections and adjustments. As humans, we encounter difficulties and mysteries that often strip our faith away. More frequent than not, that turbulence leaves us emotionally naked and vulnerable. Influenced by our older kids' grandfather from their mom's side, Silly's faith was bigger than a mustard seed. It was a faith that turned his illness, family challenges, and all the sad moments into adventures. One that made him see adversities as blessings.

Growing up with health challenges, his dream was to create a world in which no one had to feel as different as he was. Being an adult with responsibility, he tried a few times to create those fantasy worlds through building Life Action Role-Play

(LARP) communities. He wanted everyone to have time and space to be their own heroes. We had to admit, he was not quite George Lucas. At each attempt he became discouraged. For a brief moment, while adjusting to being a full-time dad and shelving his creative idea for a new world, he explored being a counselor. But the radiation treatment took his voice away for a while. It redirected him away from completing his schooling. Friends from his previous LARP community visited after his treatment. Reminiscing about their grand time, they shared how much the role-player community missed Silly's presence.

Starting reluctantly, my dear creative husband rebuilt his own LARP community. The project not only helped busy his mind but also rescued his mental state. He brought together many people with the same interests from all walks of lives. Many took part in the community as they felt different and not accepted in their "real" world. He helmed the leadership of this creative social community until shortly before he died. He gifted me with the caring group of people he left behind.

There are so many more stories about surrendering our difficulties and challenges to what was intended by something or someone greater than us. Often, we stared at the unfairness in our lives. Then we paused and accepted that when the universe decided it was ours to have at the intended time, it would become so. My journey now, just as it was with Silly, included glimmers of hope, anger, and a fair share of disappointments. I found solace in quiet mindfulness and embracing what was intended.

It's okay to be sad, or happy

Furry Love

Growing up in Indonesia, I consumed dozens of handkerchiefs or a box of tissues a day, sneezing. Indonesia, an archipelago sitting on the equator, was hot and humid. My sheltered self grew up with limited exposure to the elements. When I left the temperature-controlled building, my allergy kicked up a few notches. Animal dander and dust were enemies to my sinuses and eyes. The idea of having any animal in my house was painful to think about.

Silly, on the other hand, was raised around horses and dogs. My first visit to his house was more than adventurous, to say the least. I was greeted by a big scary boxer which Silly referred to as the sweetest baby. Around the back of his house, a few giant rottweilers roamed around. Though allergy was the root cause, my lack of exposure to animals triggered fear. Dogs had been monstrous beasts to me.

When our relationship bloomed and marriage was discussed, we met in the middle about having animals in the family. Not having pets was not an option. The next choice was to have a pet that did not scare me. We started small, with a fish. That never lasted more than seven days. Then we tried a guinea pig. The furry creature spreading its dander inside the house twenty-four hours a day proved to be a nightmare. Worse, it whistled after dark. I was more than grateful when Silly suggested giving up Herbie the guinea pig. After a friend adopted the whistling hairball, he suggested a ferret. He made the mistake, however, with a joke I could not shake off months prior.

"You know what a ferret is?" he asked. I guessed it was a stinky animal. He laughed and shook his head. "A gerbil that survived."

He had to explain that to me. It was a gerbil that went up someone's bottom and came out elongated. I had my palm on my face in addition to extensive eye rolls. Therefore, no, I could not have a ferret.

I gave in and we adopted a golden retriever. We, the golden retriever and I, did not get along. Destructive was an under-statement. She caused a big scene and damage to my apart-ment. Her adoption by a friend was followed by our acqui-sition of a pug. He loved to pee on my bed when Silly was around. Another bad match.

We bought our first house before our firstborn turned one. Silly convinced me that the fenced-in backyard was waiting for something more than children. My frugality and the emp-ty new house led us to visit thrift stores and weekend markets. At the flea market one Saturday, we walked by a family with three huskies minutes before the market closed. We heard them packing and they were about to drop those babies at the rescue center. We visited them and Silly played with the two heterochromia puppies. Their different colored eyes did not sit well with me. I couldn't remember how much they wanted for them. Fixated on the third puppy, an all-white, brown-eyed timid one at the back of the kennel, I asked about her. The gentleman looked down at her. "She's all white, maybe sick, ten dollars."

I did not let go of her on the way home. We named her Anastasia, Annie for short. We had stocked up on Benadryl and all other sorts of allergy medicine since she came home with us. As years passed and after our Chub was born, we gave Annie a few more furry friends.

Annie died of organ failure when she was seventeen years old, leaving Sac the boxer and Patch, the pirate pit bull. Silly was holding me when our mobile vet came to the house to put her to sleep. I never thought I'd ever say this, but that grief was different and tugged on me harder than I thought it could. The great not-so-great thing that event taught me was how Sac and Patch displayed emotion. One Saturday when I felt lost and alone, Patch stopped eating to sit on my feet. The displayed behavior of loss; it was so pure and real.

Our home hosted family members when Silly departed for the multiverse. The day his body was moved to be cremated, among the hustle and bustle of people in and out of the house, both Patch and Sac ran away. Already swimming in pain, I couldn't describe the additional pain of losing those two. Their absence created a storm of turmoil. Both dogs were there for our son during his breakups, our daughter's job loss, and they were there especially on the day my kids lost their dad.

Every day we split up to locate them. We combed neighborhoods and relied on social media to help us. On the day the last family member left our house, my phone rang. Someone had spotted Patch by Chub's school and brought him back to us. On the third month of Silly's death, exactly to the day, a repairman left the house with our front door wide open. I remembered so vividly coming down the stairs and seeing a white dog staring at Silly's picture. I dialed my friends' phones, certain that my eyes were tricking me.

"Which one of my dogs is this?" I asked, showing a few friends on video call a white dog sitting in front of me.

They yelped, "Sac's home! He's home!" Both of the fur babies had returned at the times I needed them the most.

Never in my wildest dreams did I think I'd lean on furry creatures to comfort me in my darkest moments. My allergy persisted while my armored ice-cold heart melted. I had to brace myself for a few more painful moments when we had to send off Sac and Patch merely within months of each other during my healing journey.

As I sat down to pen this chapter, three gray cats were chasing each other across our living room and a cream-colored Siamese laid across my lap. Silly often said "Animals are the best nanny! They will always be there for our kids after we're gone." Indeed.

*I hope you are wrapped
in love*

Honey Do's

Our histories, health challenges, and blended family made me believe that we were one of the modern family pioneers. The day before his pneumonectomy was the last time he could work. He was crushed. For each medical happening, we adapted. With a total of four little humans at home, we made the decision for him to stay home and be the super dad that he was. He became the loving figure, the enforcer of discipline, and the ever-reliable "kids' taxi." In the meantime, breaking the housewife tradition, I ventured out to work and provide for the household. Our roles diverged from the mainstream. Our flexible dynamic allowed each of us to thrive in our respective domains while supporting one another in an unconventional partnership.

There were days I felt overwhelmed, starting the day off rough and disarranging my peace. I always knew I could count on his constant support. Just a phone call away, he'd listen patiently. When I sighed my relief, he would simply say, "Give me a list of what you need to do so you can relax when you get home." Our practical moments created a safety net that caught the pieces of my hectic day.

We were never perfect. There were also days when he had his more selfish and childish moments. He would instigate my fussiness. My annoyance would bubble over. I often had to remind him of those sweet days when help was freely offered. The response I received was never what I wanted. Nonchalantly he often said, "I am not made that way. If you want me to do it, send me a daily honey-do list and I will try my best." That always turned my frown upside down. The sincerely casual response helped me realize that love comes in various forms. Some required a bit of guidance, a list, to brew into actions that touch the heart, my heart.

Many weekends I had to redo tasks that were hastily completed during the busy week. The dishes may not have sparkled the way I preferred. The broom wasn't stowed in its proper place. Small discrepancies frequently sparked friction between us. As our partnership matured, so did our understanding and tolerance. I learned to appreciate his efforts. I became accustomed to his best and his great intentions. If I felt the need to rewash a dish or straighten the broom, it was my choice, one I made for my own satisfaction. It was not a reflection of his inadequacy. Eventually, we accepted the ebbs and flows of our modern household routine. At the end of the day, everything worked out just fine.

It's been a while since I've written a honey-do list, for neither him nor us. Standing by the sink full of dishes, the noticeable void from his absence brought reminiscing moments of our playful domestic dynamic. Those lists were more than reminders; they were a translation of varied love languages. A testament of the priceless, gentle fussing and affectionate bossing. I began to make lists for myself. Beyond organizing tasks, I did it to also cherish the warmth that still lingers from the teasing love we shared. What partnership meant was understood beyond words.

Share your feelings

School Bus Hero

A new routine ensued with Peep started taking the bus to school. Silly would sit in his hammock with baby Chub. Facing the bus stop shortly after he had his lunch, they would wait. Around three p.m. the bus stopped one house down. Little Man and Peep would get off the bus and walk hand in hand toward the house. Video calling, one of the greatest bits of technology, helped me experience a few of these moments while I worked.

My desk phone rang one afternoon. There was the sound of panic on the other side. "The bus did not stop!" I could hear Silly panting.

My heart stopped. He hung up the phone after letting me know his plan. I was home an hour or so later and found my brood all there, safe and sound. The air was different, but they were all smiles. Silly and I stepped out onto the porch, and he told me, "The assistant principal called me to come get them at the school." I recalled my confusion. He continued, "Little Man always sits next to Peep on the bus. When he got on the bus today a girl was already sitting next to her. Peep was scared." Quoting the assistant principal, he said, "Your son said 'get the fuck up! I sit next to my sister.'"

Making sure no little eyes were watching us from inside the house, we both laughed. The school administration decided not to suspend our son for his courage to protect his sister. Our only task was to let him know not to use that word on school property.

My Silly always instilled goodness in our children since I knew him. He encouraged their do-unto-others behavior since before they could clean their own bottoms. I was not a fan of the use of what I thought then was an offensive word. His wise explanation was: "We can tell them when and where to use it, but we can't shelter them. They will hear and use the word; it's best we know and teach them how." Regardless, we were both proud of Little Man's courage to protect his sister.

One of the last conversations Silly and I had was about the rampant pride for mediocrity in the world. I was raised to appreciate participation awards. Being a parent, especially partnering with a wise man, my perspective changed. Our pride for our children and the human beings they were becoming surpassed any tangible awards. Little Man's action was prompt, chivalrous. Many may prefer to punish him for bad words, but to us, his action trumped what he said.

We applied that wisdom to many things. I felt safe with Silly there guiding our children in becoming purposeful warriors through his life and his everlasting wisdom. Oversharing was not a word we used. Free speech was upheld in our house within respectful boundaries. The world rewarded all actions of kindness. It brought a sense of pride and calm when my son recently told an acquaintance to not speak to his mom, me, disrespectfully. Silly lived through the children being there for

each other, defending each other's honor, and becoming re-
sources in their time of needs. They were my young warriors.

You are stranger than you know

Lunch Dates

"Oh, don't drink that!" Silly snatched the hot sauce bottle Chub had squeezed and turned the bottom up toward her mouth.

That was not the first time our mischievously curious Chub tried to drink hot sauces at restaurants we visited. When she was the only one at home, Silly started a sweet routine of getting out of the house, something he could do often when he worked. He made time for a quick ice cream stop with the baby, or walk to the bookstore where he met people who shared his interests. Some other days, he would have lunch with the other children.

During some random moments he began to visit me at work with our mini-me in tow. His visits changed me and my bad habit of not having a work break. During those visits, he would drag me out of my working lunch to get some sun and have my midday me time. This simple act lit up our energy outside the confines of our transformed home and the brick-and-mortar office. It was a poignant reminder of balance.

When we plunged into having our nontypical family unit, there were moving parts without routines and tradition. It was pure proof to the unconventionally resilient patterns of love and support. After Chub started school, the rhythm of Silly's unexpected visits didn't waver. He intertwined his new routine with our week. They became bright spots on otherwise ordinary days. I often found myself eagerly waiting for those work breaks. Our spontaneous midday dates brought us smiles, laughter, and reconnections. Even when money was tight, we held onto this cherished new tradition. We would celebrate our time in the simplicity of a ninety-nine cent hot-dog lunch. The value of our time together far outweighed the price of the meal.

Something about having hot dogs for a meal alone brought the sweet memories of when we spent thirty minutes across from each other. For those precious minutes, we were transported away from our worries. We immersed ourselves in a world where laughter and conversation were the only things that truly mattered. The memory taught me balance and how adjustments were all right. Through all the changes in our time together, we made it! Joy remained no matter the price.

Chub began to drive herself to school two years after Silly's death. Celebrating the memory of those lunch dates, I began to have moments for quick bites with her. When school was off, she would come to my work with food. Sitting across from her, away from my computer for thirty minutes to an hour, I hoped to instill in her a value of cherished moments. And every so often I reminded her of the time she attempted to drink the hot sauce.

Have yourself your
favorites

A Droplet Makes Waves

Silly's kindness was not just a part of him, it was what drew others in, including me. His magnetic and intoxicating kindness made him the sexy being he was. It overshadowed his charming smile and piercing blue eyes. What clicked within our couplehood was our parallel goal to spread the kindness we knew to the world. We both acknowledged the need to challenge the darkness with acts of goodness and compassion. Our different lives led us both to believe the smallest gestures could make big changes. Every thoughtful and selfless act, and moments of empathy, contributed to the wave of transformation we wanted to create.

In each of our struggles, we experienced unique kindness. Though what we received was varied and specific to each of us, we both agreed to pay them forward just the same.

One nice weekend, we took the brood to our favorite Chinese brunch place in the nearby city. The establishment was in a run-down parking lot. The fragmented pavement and pile of broken cement blocks caused the kids to say we had entered a warzone. As we finished our meal and buckled in to leave, a disheveled lady came up to us. Standing among the potholes, she asked if we could spare some cash. She painted her desperation for medicine money against the backdrop of a pharmacy across the street. I was skeptical, but without hesitation, Silly took out his wallet. He handed her the last bit of cash he had. Our Booger Bear protested.

"She would probably use it for cigarettes or drugs," Booger Bear proclaimed.

Silly smiled and replied, "My kindness is my action; what they do with it is up to them."

A powerful conviction of kindness and sincerity.

For a moment he drove in silence. With grace, he taught us a lesson that echoed our values forever. My memory retained the expression on his face and the look on each of my children's faces. Often when life got tough, the memory of that moment grounded me. In that unspoken exchange, empathy filled their young eyes.

One evening after his guys' night out, Silly told me that he wanted to be a knight. I chuckled and thought he had had a bit much to drink. His serious tone stopped me from what I was doing so I could listen. He passionately shared how he and a few friends valued ancient chivalry and believed they could bring it into the modern world.

Silly and his friends wanted to channel their anger, sadness, and hate to better themselves, each other, and their community. The transformation of the brotherhood was not only personal to them; it touched everyone around them. They became beacons of positive change, spreading kindness and support wherever they went.

His journey to be the knight he envisioned was not a walk in the park. Many people saw him as weird, some with admiration, and a lot with curiosity. He faced raised eyebrows and stifled laughs at social gatherings, his old friends struggling to understand his newfound chivalrous pursuits. But he did not let that stop him. His determination was as strong as the steel he admired. What they didn't understand was that his quest became an emblem of aspiring to a life filled with virtue and honor at a time when those ideals seemed like relics of the past.

His kind heart was especially passionate about fighting child hunger in our community. Our family embraced this mission. Multiple times a year, we would load up our car with nonperishable food items and the kids' favorite snacks to distribute.

"We live in a wealthy country, it breaks my heart to know that there are so many hungry children," Silly often said with both disbelief and determination. "It's our responsibility to help change that."

His declining health during the couple of years approaching the end of his journey brought discomfort. The unbearable pain, both physically and emotionally, had him retreat from social settings. People glared at him when he sat in the car while I loaded groceries. They spoke unkindly when he couldn't sit on the bleachers for the kids' sports games for too long. He took in the blows from rudeness and inconsiderate statements. Nonetheless, every chance he had, he practiced only kindness. His actions, though unnoticed by most, were filled with the same deep love and compassion. From the confines of his own struggles, his heart reached out.

In the stretch of time I have seen his service to the world, he also did some acts of kindness in silence and without any audience. Preparing his memorial, I received a few letters from acquaintances. *He saved my life*, one said. They did not speak to each other often. At an intuitive moment, my Silly called them to say what they meant to him. Like a rescue route, Silly pulled them out of a crisis. I knew he was being rewarded wherever he was.

As I swam in the sea of darkness to find healing, I found comfort in unexpected acts of kindness from many people. It was as if his kindness to others returned to me when I needed it most. There were times when complete strangers offered helping hands the way he used to. Other times, they said something so comforting just when I felt the most alone. I couldn't help but think that this was his spiritual influence reaching out to me through them. I was convinced it was his spirit fostering compassion and showing that his legacy of love continued to touch the lives of others.

The memory of Silly's big heart had me channeling my sense of loss into making a conscious effort to lend a helping hand more often, too. The harder I struggled, the more I strived to be a blessing to others. The spirit of generosity he instilled in me had become a guiding principle. It inspired me to seek out new ways to assist and serve others in my daily life. Every smile I received in return became a toast, a celebration. Integrity should never be measured by guaranteed outcomes and praises. It is defined by the purity of intentions. Forever and always, I knew that day he placed a pillar of character within our kids. Many days I prayed that wherever he was, he saw how that moment had shaped our children's kind hearts and generosity to the world.

Celebrate kindness

Relocated South

Our wedding was a simple affair, with every detail reflecting simplicity. I made a floral headpiece that added a touch of nature to my look, and my self-designed dress flowed elegantly, despite its humble origin. My sandals, a find from a forgotten store, carried me lightly as if I were walking on Middle-earth itself. In the embrace of an old forest, we declared our love in a ceremony inspired by Tolkien's fantasy world, paying tribute to the tales that mirrored our bond and the adventures that awaited us.

Lady Galadriel's ethereal beauty in Tolkien's film adaptations left a lasting impression, but I knew my wedding attire needed a personal touch. Taking inspiration from her, I designed my dress to be timeless and adaptable to life's changes. It was cut in a flowing style that would always flatter my figure, whether fuller or slimmer, ensuring I would look back on our wedding day with fondness. The fabric whispered promises of future tales, as I imagined what our daughters might achieve. I crafted the dress with an adjustable hem, hoping they might one day wear it on each of their own wedding days, symbolizing the vows their parents made.

A decade after the birth of our spirited, jumbo-sized baby girls, a whimsical desire took hold of me. I wanted to wear the dress again, to feel its embrace and reflect on how life had reshaped me. With anticipation, I put it on, expecting to see the dress fitting perfectly, accentuating my fuller figure. But as I stood in front of the mirror, something felt off about the impeccably tailored dress. Tears welled in my eyes; had I over-looked something in my crafting? I thought I had designed the laced back to fit me in any size. The girls helped me pull, tug, and adjust, and still, the dress was off. Seeking comfort, I turned to Silly, torn between distress and hope.

The printed fiction in his hand occupied his focus. Silly glanced up and met my gaze, and with a reassuring grin, he teased, "Honey, they've relocated south."

At that moment, I was torn between laughter and tears, torn between his jest and the unfamiliarity of the dress. But as his laughter mingled with mine, tears of relief and joy streamed down our faces.

"You should be happy, you never thought you'd have any boobs," his teasing continued.

Reminding me of my youthful insecurities, they now seemed trivial. His words brought comfort, confirming that the only flaw in my carefully crafted design was the inabili-ty to predict this great change. It was a sweet affirmation, a reminder that change is a natural part of life's journey. Some parts of me may travel south while others drift from east to west, but these transitions are okay.

As the dawn broke following my dark moments of grief, I resolved to begin a journey of rediscovering myself. Starting with small acts of self-care, I put color to my withered and muted self. Despite his complete love for everything that I was, I struggled to find myself again. I decided to infuse my monotonous existence with vibrant colors in my hair and my outfits. In the calm of the evening, I prepared myself for the next day, a ritual of readiness. Into the mirror, I affirmed my promise to face the world with a renewed outlook. I resurrected the forgotten aspects of myself that had been buried under the weight of grieving life. The slight curl I put in my hair and the thin eyeliner around my eyes removed the expected chaos of the day ahead. In its place was a fresh start. The reborn ritual that set me on my path of self-discovery.

Under a sky full of stars, I stood embracing all the changes. I surrounded myself with a deep stillness. Silly reflected his pure and genuine love that touched my soul in a way no words could describe. He accepted my unfiltered thoughts and my true self. During the time we spent together, we both changed physically. He never cared about the little wrinkles on my clothes and around my eyes. I never cared when cancer radiation changed him into a size smaller than mine, and his heart failure put all the weight back on him, and more. It was a love with no conditions, no need for any facades. Just a warm embrace for every part of me, past and present. Love never wavered. It simply grew to embrace every contour of ourselves.

To the universe, I released my thanks. I would be forever grateful for his gift of serenity and his loving me wholeheartedly. His embrace held the beauty in accepting myself as I was. The inner splendor that resonated in my soul radiated for myself and others. To my children, I spoke often of loving themselves as they were. Change is a human thing.

Welcome change

Pumpkin, Spruce, and Bergamot

I married a man with an amazing aura around him, adored and loved by so many. Silly was a real magnet for attention, especially from the ladies. They, just like I, were captivated by his social skills, emotional intelligence, and those gorgeous deep blue eyes that seemed to hold a thousand stories.

Seemingly different and occasionally small next to him, I misplaced my confidence often when I was known to otherwise be alone. Many days, fear-infused jealousy surfaced. When I verbalized my emotion, he responded with such tenderness. A simple kiss on my forehead or sometimes just a silly face instantly brightened up even the gloomiest mood. "You still give me butterflies," he would confess.

The sincere and kind voice made my heart skip a beat. His love was a constant promise in the ocean of chaos, my Silly, my North Star during those moments of doubt.

After a decade together, he understood that I was not like those lavender or cucumber-melon girls. I was all about pumpkin spice, spruce, and bergamot. While others sought comfort in the familiar, he encouraged me to embrace my uniqueness and stand out from the crowd. For all my quirks and weirdness, he never once asked me to change. "Those quirks make you who you are," he told me.

It wasn't easy embracing my uniqueness in a world that often prefers conformity. My parents, traditional at heart, found my peculiar tastes and passions confusing. Our differences led to misunderstandings and a divide between us. Their perspective, painted in proper pastel shades of conventionality, clashed with my vibrant mosaic of individuality.

The phrase *I think the neighbor thinks I am rocking the cradle from the internet* became a running joke when we first settled in our first ever house. Passing down our unique personas to our children, we made a garden mixture of characters. Our family did not lack glares and stares. As they entered the intricacy of early adulthood, their vibrant threads also took on shades of distinction. Amazing humans they all are with each of their own unique style and personality. They, too, experienced unkindness. Silly's cheers encouraged them to always shine in their own originality. "Be true to yourself, don't blend in, you are made to stand out," he would often tell them.

His passionate advocates lifted them. The power of believing in the strength of character and the brilliance of their unique personalities took root. Their dad never ceased to remind us that what others thought was just a passing whisper was a symphony of our own unique melody. Good ol' dad's wisdom was sunshine to the garden where not everything was the same.

Becoming a single mom, I had big shoes to fill. Providing comfort and strength to my children who faced the cruelty of being bullied through their various adolescent years rocked me. I hung on to his wisdom to support them with love and understanding. Brazing the challenge, I offered them the strength of a pumpkin, the resilience of a spruce, and the uplifting essence of bergamot.

Though it pained me to witness their struggles, my heart beamed with pride as they held steadfast to their convictions of what was right and wrong. In a field of the mundane, they stood out brightly, unwavering in their beliefs. When in doubt, our children leaned on true courage where their values lay, especially in the face of adversity. I hoped to be an example, a living proof of embracing one's individuality. It was in this acceptance and diverse soil, that their vibrant and nonconforming souls flourished, shining their extraordinary colors in a world that often lacks diversity.

Wear your favorite outfit today

Promise To Keep

Death was not a topic we avoided. We acknowledged it as a natural part of life, an inevitable end to every human journey. However, this stoic mindset did not fully prepare me for its harsh reality. It was a crash course on accepting life's harsh truths. I believed my partner, a survivor of many challenges and health scares, was invincible. Secretly, I thought fate would pick me first, in a twist of irony. Yet, his resilient spirit only strengthened our determination to cherish every moment we had.

As we grew older together, our faces became adorned with wrinkles from shared laughter and tears. His fortieth birthday was a milestone; he'd lived over two decades more than what the doctor had told to his mother. In his infrequent serious looks he said, "If you die before me, I won't marry again. I mean, who would want me, right?" I rolled my eyes each time he said it then dismissed his unnecessary worry. Lightheartedly Silly always continued with, "You can do anything you want, as long as you promise me to be happy. When you're happy, I am happy, no matter where I am." It was a promise that added a silver lining to the fabric of our future goodbyes.

As my memory replayed them, those words sounded vastly different now then when he was by my side. It was easy for me to nod to the statement when I could turn to snuggle with him after. I would honor our love by embracing the potential for joy in life, someday.

On my way home from work before the life-changing day, I felt a weird pang in my chest. It was an unsettling tug that seemed to call out Silly's name. Fear blanketed me. I raced up the stairs with tears streaming down my face when I reached home. He was waking up from a nap, and without thinking twice, I hugged him tight. I buried my face in his chest. My tears mixed with snot didn't matter. I pleaded, "Please, never ever leave me, ever," over and over again. He laughed! To my surprise and relief, his laughter wasn't dismissive but affectionate. He cradled my head, lifting my gaze so our eyes locked, a serene kindness in his.

"I can't believe you're crying over me like I'm gone," he teased gently, brushing away my tears. With a firm certainty that bolstered my heart, he added, "No matter what happens, I'll always be with you." A silent vow hung in the air, a promise that the inevitable couldn't break.

Months went by when I attempted my journey to move forward. A revised life without his physical presence. I held onto his promise and continued my hope to see him through the interconnected fabric of the universe. There was nothing but a stark world. The absence of whispered secrets and shared laughter was loud. My heart searched for him in the rustling leaves, the bustling crowds, the peaceful solitude of dawn, but I found nothing. There I was, left to explore a world that used to be filled with his love, now empty and gloomy.

On one of my heavy days, all caught up in work, the kids, and house chores, I noticed things only he would do, say, or know. The kids would burst into laughter, a sound so much like his own. The wind would carry a distant conversation with his tone of voice. All those fragmented pieces of our past often stopped me in my tracks. Bitter and sweet they reminded me that a part of him still lived on around us. Even the creak of the third step as I climbed the stairs at night, which used to annoy me when he climbed them, now felt like our little secret code. The ways he found to stay connected to the small details of our everyday life were subtle and mysterious. It was such an assurance to me that love truly had its own everlasting presence in the rituals he left behind.

He was keeping his promise, the best that this puzzling universe allowed. They were nuggets of comfort. Our memories intertwined with the present, creating a tapestry of his lasting legacy. Our love story did not end. He had always been here, woven into the fabric of our lives.

Keep moving forward

Anger Does Not Sleep On Our Bed

Coming home from full workdays, or while parenting, various big emotions joined us in bed often. I was the worst of the both of us, often taking frustration to bed and waking up on the wrong side of it. The snowball effect wreaked only havoc. After years of tripping over each other's emotions, we made our pact to never go to bed angry, and we agreed that anger wouldn't be our silent bedfellow, wedged between us to ruin our nights. Verbalizing our feelings effortlessly became a part of our relationship. This understanding became our safe haven, a respected practice that made room for honest conversations and diffused conflicts with heartfelt communication. We never went to bed without resolving our differences; we valued the peace that came from ending the day with forgiveness rather than lingering unrest.

Our younger two, Chub and Peep, slept with us until they were close to three feet tall. The older two, Booger Bear and Little Man, loved surprise visitations without knocking. We often joked about the miracle of having our youngest at all with our inability to evict the kids from our beds. Looking back, those nights of having some, if not all of the kids gathered around in our room, were priceless.

Our conversations got even more interesting as we got older. With our bodies expanded from all the ice cream and donuts we shared throughout the years, he joked, "Our kids may have moved out of our bed, but we've also gotten wider. There's just no room for anger here." It was Silly's subtle remark, accompanied by a chuckle, that softened the reality around us. His humor was a gentle reminder that our bond was not just about the absences, but also about the space we filled, both literally and metaphorically.

The physical closeness our age and indulgence brought us highlighted a deeper truth. As our boundaries blurred and merged, any space that anger could occupy was lovingly crowded out by shared laughter and a lifetime of sweet, simple moments.

When waves of anger welled up inside me, I couldn't help but feel frustrated. He was not here to guide me through the challenges with our kids. A script of wisdom on how to calm their storms was absent in my time of need. Lately, I learned to find comfort sitting on the edge of our bed. I hissed out all my inner turmoil, giving my feelings some air and acknowledging how heavy they were.

At the end of my frustrated rant, I whispered fervently into the quiet of our room, "I know you'll keep your promise to be here in spirit. I'll look for you in the moments we share, and I'll listen for your guidance. Please, help me figure this out. I am not going to bed angry."

The backdrop of my grief was a messy, chaotic ball of emotions. In this emotional maze, one feeling stood out: anger. It was like a fire that sometimes fueled me, sometimes consumed me. I could feel it coursing through me, demanding attention, in stark contrast to the passive sadness that often comes with loss. But as I navigated through this mix of emotions, I learned to ride its waves, using its energy to honor his memory instead of letting it overshadow the love we shared.

Sleep well. Love

The Legacy of Love

"**A**re you going to eat the rest of your noodles? If not I will." Silly stopped mid-sentence when I said that.

He pushed his half-full bowl toward me and continued talking about the two kids he loved so very much. That was our first lunch date. I did not know it would be the first of many. People around us may have thought we were on a modified speed-dating night, and I was listening to his entire life which he freely shared while I ate. His health resume included his birth defect, motorcycle accidents, and cancer at that point. He was not shy about his mental health, his brokenness, and his faith. Best of all, however, was how he beamed with pride talking about his two children. That same moment, he learned about my love for food and how I fit the entirety of stereotypical Asian females. We met each other's puzzle pieces. Though I was shrouded in fear of losing him to his health and becoming a step-mom, that day I knew that we were meant to do great things together.

When I was little, my cousin, Irma, asked me if I would choose to love a handsome-but-broken man, or a not-so-handsome man with a perfect life. Silly was my Aladdin, my beautiful diamond in the rough, very *very* rough. We met each other's brokenness with laughter. Many things we disagreed on, except our faith and kind purpose. Halfway through our journey together, we started finishing each other's sentences. Preemptively prepared for each other's frustration, we welcomed apologies and moments to speak our minds.

"You are my weird-shaped puzzle piece," he said to me once, and he was mine.

It was his time to take the morning medicine when Chub and I found him unresponsive on his recovery bed, the one the kids set up in my office. The glimpse of hope when the paramedic arrived and rushed him to the hospital died when they ushered us into a small private waiting room. Shortly after the doctor confirmed he was gone, I sat frozen on the passenger seat as my friend took me home from the hospital. Climbing up the stairs at our house was mountainous. A mix of cries and giggles echoed through the hallway. All four kids had gathered on one of their beds. Red-faced and puffy-eyed, they made space for me to join them without saying a word. They kept sharing their special moments with their dad.

"Dad is an organ donor right?" one of them asked. Looking back on it, those first hours and days were such a blur, I couldn't begin to tell you who asked the question.

"Yep! But every part of him has been broken since he was born, I don't think anyone would want any of it," I replied. All laughed. Their hands interlinked, all four of them together.

"I get no respect!" Little Man said, mimicking their dad. All four of them roared with laughter.

They were not wrong. His birth defect resulted in his lung removal at the age of thirty. An accident he had years before we met had put steel up and down his body. His cancer treatments, two of them by the time he died, had wreaked havoc with his upper body organs. Not to mention the final sign of his body's tiredness with the heart failure.

At one point, I struggled to hold back my laughter, followed by a burst of tears. "It's okay to laugh, Mom," Peep said, wise beyond her years, "Dad would want you to keep laughing. He left us with amazing memories."

And that he did. Before the day ended, we received confirmation that two people would be receiving his corneas so they could see.

We sent him off in his kilt, his knighthood tabard, and his sword nestled next to him. We gathered for a toast under the clear night sky. Jupiter shone brightly among the dark clouds in the night sky and chaperoned us as we shared his favorite pepperoni pie and kegged lager. The tree of life carved into the wooden chest where his remains rested sat centered on an altar. Long past that day, we celebrated a life fully lived. Tirelessly, the kids and I reminded each other of the challenges their dad courageously completed.

Like the river traveling among the boulders, my journey forward navigated through detours and sudden changes. Saddened by the news of friends losing their partners, I was grateful that they came to me for comfort. Their need for me were touches I needed from the universe. Each of us still walked in our own uncertainties, but we strode forward with strength just the same. Each story shared represented both my obstacles and my new journey. They exposed the voids and grace of the vibrant life we had created together. Love and laughter can be had even in his physical absence. They are the legacy of our love from day one.

Into the morning air I whispered, "Hey, good morning." I hope it reached him somehow, somewhere. "I love you," I said. I held onto the invisible thread that connected us across time and space with those words. Often the soft touch of the morning breeze echoed *I love you too.*

Wherever he was, even in the unseen realms, our shared journey continued on.

I love you

Epilogue

Every morning since the day he drifted to the multiverse, I wake up to a different silence. The undisturbed blankets next to me present a void of the warmth I long for. Gratefulness settles in when anguish and pain propel me to swim with my memories. Ones that surface to heal.

No matter where you are on your spiritual journey, we are all interconnected. Each inhale reminds us that we are integral parts of a larger world. Knowing that our loved ones remain part of this grand tapestry, as do we, brings comfort in times of loss. Nature's cycles mirror our own experiences of highs and lows, presence and absence. It is never-ending as we balance holding on and letting go.

The journey through grief leaves bruises and an ache that no words can truly describe. Allow the raw pain and scars to provide an honest reflection that embraces both the challenges and triumphs of life after loss. We don't have to go through it alone. We can be traveling buddies, sharing experiences, finding community, and drawing strength from the daily rising of the sun.

There's no one-size-fits-all to the grief healing process. Society often expects a linear path to recovery. Sometimes, we might seem rude or short-tempered, unintentionally hurting those around us with our pain. Part of healing is having the grace to apologize and recognizing these moments as part of our journey. It's an ongoing process that allows us to ride the waves of emotions until we're ready to find solid ground.

I hope *Good Morning, I Love You* lights up some glow. Grief is the price we pay for love. Though it often feels unbelievable, there is joy beneath it all. The opportunity to have loved and be loved is an extraordinary gift. Our hearts are never alone. Take what brings smiles to our faces and peace to our souls. Leave behind what feels completely foreign. Allow ourselves to truly feel our own stories.

For those who have experienced loss and refuse to lose themselves in the process, embrace what lies ahead. For all those working on intertwining stories and making the best of memories, do not hold back.

"Even when we're apart, I'll always be with you," Pooh whispered to Christopher Robin, a gentle reminder that love knows no bounds, not even those of space and time. It's in this enduring sentiment we find the true essence of connection.

It takes a village to raise a child, they say. I say it takes a village to live. Death is the closing parenthesis to all life, with many words to follow. When that next word is spoken, the village changes. Some stay, some go, and everything changes along with it.

When the day begins with dread, allow me to say this to you daily:

Good morning, I love you.

You are no longer alone in this journey.

Never alone.

About the author

Born and raised in Central Java, Indonesia, V is the youngest and most chaotically artistic of three children. She moved to the US as a student at the University of Michigan in Ann Arbor and has lived in North Carolina since 2000 where she began her life-changing journey as a wife, stepmother, mother, friend, professional, and recently an artist.

Empowered by a diverse technical background and the profound life experience of navigating grief and the complexities of raising a unique family, V has been called to connect with others through shared vulnerabilities. She hopes to offer solace and understanding, creating a beacon of hope and companionship for those facing life's myriad challenges with her writing.

Next from the heart and pen of V Rose:

Sweet Dream, Beautiful: Self-Rediscovery After Loss through Healing and Courageous Transformation

In the calm of the evening, my sense of loss is magnified, every shadow echoing the emptiness. In the same breath, it's in this velvety darkness that I can freely delve into my thoughts and emotions, away from daytime distractions. The night turns into a trusted companion and a formidable foe, welcoming my deepest reflections and battling waves of sorrow. Moments for contemplation and self-rediscovery, a task with a bitter-sweet price.

You're So Weird, Mom: A Personal Adventure of a Courageously Weird Widow and Single Parent

Life itself is unpredictable. Life after the loss of a partner with children involved is hilariously unpredictable, requiring strides in the chaos of widowhood, parenthood, and the wild ride that is life itself. It is for the strong-minded and opinion-ated single parents who march to the beat of our own drums.

Special Thanks To

Khedron de Leon for the initial read and confidence in me.

Lisa Camichos for enabling me to trust myself and do more.

Keva Graphics for the longtime friendship and help with the amazing cover.

Cami Hepler for the pre-delivery edits and excitement on my stories.

For the Rose "Framily" for allowing me to lean on all of you through my time of healing.